GREEN WHITE GREED

A Play

'FEMI AWOLESI

GREEN WHITE GREED

To the human heart depraved,

To the human heart deprived,

To the human heart depressed,

To the human heart despaired.

CHARACTERS

NARRATOR

ENGEE

YOBA

IGO

KOG

HASA

BENI

MR. WAI

ABLE-BODIED MEN

DANCERS

PASSERSBY

GRADE I

There is a slow but deep humming in the background. Deep enough to stir up absolute serenity in the audience. Able-bodied men soon carry a corpse to the center stage. The corpse is wrapped in green and white. They gently place the corpse down, face each other in twos, and exit. IGO enters, weeping bitterly. He walks to the corpse, speaking in a native language.

IGO

My mother, my mother! My source!

My beloved Engee!

Why did you leave me?

Why did you leave us?

Without you I have no name of mine,

No place to live in.

Solace is not seen,

No place to call my home.

I cannot be welcomed anywhere else

Like you always did,

You nurtured me,

With you was peace and solace,

But we turned deaf ear.

Look at me here.

I resisted your instructions,

I showed no compassion,

I became the shadow of death

And the rainbow of dearth,

Like a broken-winged bird

That cannot fly,

So am I;

Naked and ashamed!

(Keeps wailing)

(Enter YOBA, HASA, BENI and KOG wailing and in turn speaking the same thing as IGO in their respective languages. Able-bodied men enter and then carry the corpse away. More wailing is heard. Enter NARRATOR, looking pitifully.)

NARRATOR

She was gunned,

And she's gone,

Far gone,

And it's widespread.

Engee is dead!

None saw this coming at the inception,

But for the deception

All soon became troubled

And now assemble

In painful reception.

She's dead and confirmed;

Left with no head,

Having had five children or perhaps more.

What a pity!

Only if they had listened;

They neglected instructions

And embraced destruction.

(NARRATOR makes as if to exit but turns back and faces the audience.)

NARRATOR

Few years ago…

(Exit NARRATOR)

GRADE II

Continuous drumming and dancing depicting an atmosphere of celebration. ENGEE; a woman dressed in white gown with a green crown, wrist-beads and necklace is sitting on the throne merrily watching the troupe of dancers display. Enter IGO, YOBA, HASA, BENI and KOG, joining the dance troupe in enthusiasm, for an eon. The dance troupe then leaves the stage; IGO, YOBA, HASA, BENI and KOG prostrate at the feet of ENGEE, and then sit on the mat. The drum is beaten to initiate silence.

ENGEE

(Softly)

My children, you know how I so much love you;

Your being birthed by me was not a mistake,

It's what God himself wanted and allowed.

It might look strange now,

But the truth is,

It is not strange to God

That you are all from me;

All the same but different,

In tongues and wit.

Only ensure this;

That these gifts do not shift you aside,

That these gifts do not drift you from me.

These gifts should lift you,

And this will not cease to exist

When you embrace oneness

Even in the midst of darkness.

You're noble,

Refuse to be robbed

Of this inherent value.

I am strong because of you;

You are strong because of me.

You are my compatriots;

Do arise forever

To this call of destiny,

Obey and make me proud.

I know as long as you will to do,

God will direct your noble cause.

You are all bound in freedom

Because of me,

But do not use this freedom in vain,

My noble children.

(IGO, YOBA, HASA, BENI and KOG nod in acceptance.)

YOBA

(With sheer seriousness and confidence)

Engee, our beloved mother;

We shall make you proud

And I can say it loud.

We cannot change where we come from,

For you remain our Source.

Without you,

Without allegiance to you,

We can never be resourceful.

We shall win together,

In summer or winter;

Whether the weather be wet,

Whether forever we sweat;

We shall win together,

Within and without.

(IGO, HASA, BENI and KOG nod in agreement and in turn convey the same speech in their respective languages. They embrace one another, and then Engee, together.)

ALL but ENGEE

(In English)

We shall always make you proud!

GRADE III

MR. WAI; bespectacled, equipped with a few techno-gadgets and a heavy backpack explores the stage for some time.

MR. WAI

(Cheerfully)

What a land so fertile!

After a travailing travel.

How I marvel

At the level of richness

I am yet to unearth.

(Crooks and uses one of the gadgets to examine the ground)

I now see why I'm here.

(Gets up and becomes briefly pensive)

I have seen no humans

Since I journeyed to the land,

Crossing that river

Several miles,

A while ago;

River Miles.

(Smiles wryly)

Yes, no humans

Apart from monkeys

With no tails.

(Brings out the binoculars from the bag and views through)

Yeah, here;

All I see again

Are monkeys with no tails.

Might they be citizens of the land?

(Undoes viewing and wears the binoculars around his neck, then gazes at the ground)

I sense gold here.

(Examines the spot with one of the gadgets and makes a cross sign on it)

What a blessed land!

GRADE IV

IGO, YOBA, HASA, BENI and KOG at the market. YOBA is weaving attire. IGO has receptacles full of gari, rice and beans in front of him. HASA is sitting by a pen of three cows. KOG is standing by a tray of akara balls. BENI is decorated with multiple beads. Each speaks in his unique language.

ALL

(In unison)

Come and buy!

Come and buy!

I have what you want,

You will come again!

I sell your best taste!

(IGO going upstage)

HASA

(To IGO, in English with native accent)

Where are you going?

                              IGO

                          (Turns, smiling)

You know me, brother.

I scarcely await customers and consumers;

I fetch them.

                             HASA

Yes, that's true.

Well, I thought you would go pee.

                             BENI

                          (To IGO)

Please tell them I sell beads,

Should they be interested.

                             HASA

                          (To IGO)

I have their kind of meat, *wallahi.*

                             YOBA

                          (To IGO)

My *aso-oke* fabrics are the latest trend.

                             KOG

                          (To IGO)

You see how fresh the balls are, right?

IGO

I hear you all,

I'll tell them all.

(Exits with a bowl of gari)

GRADE V

Same day. IGO trying to persuade passersby.

IGO

You need food to survive,

I sell all kinds of food stuff;

I package good health.

In case you haven't heard,

My food is the best on earth.

Taste this one for free,

Please taste.

(Offers passersby bowl of gari but they ignore. Puts some in his mouth.)

This is sweet,

Truth to God.

Look, I sell other things too;

I sell *aso-oke,*

I sell sweet akara balls,

Get healthy cows for your rites,

My beads will make you a new bride.

(None answers still, and he is left in solitude. He sits faintly on the ground in deep thought and laments afterwards.)

IGO

Today of all days, why!

(In native language)

Why isn't there any sale today?

MR. WAI

(Emerges from behind)

Hey!

(Faces IGO. Offers his hand but he's ignored. He sits next to IGO.)

You must be Engee's son.

IGO

(In English with native accent)

I am not in the mood, please!

Don't get me pissed,

I am not at peace.

How dare you ask such,

When you know that Engee has not only one child

But numerous children?

I wonder why you are still here,

I thought you only came to explore,

To see how savvy and curvy our women are,

Just that we'll leave them to no stranger,

After all you got rings on your fingers;

Your white lady trusts you enough

To have let you sojourn singly.

MR. WAI

Well, true.

Your women are pretty and inviting,

But I think all that your people need

Is a banana.

And you know, it's never black here.

(IGO gets up and tries to strangle MR. WAI who shudders and pleas. IGO sits back in fury.)

MR. WAI

I was only pulling your leg.

I thought you were friends with me.

Anyway, I am sorry.

(Brief silence)

You look gloomy,

I have not seen you this way before,

Except now.

                          IGO

Mr. Wai,

I cannot fathom why

Today of all days

I made no profit.

                      MR. WAI

Really? So sad.

If I may ask,

How much profit do you make in a day?

                          IGO

Well… like twenty thousand.

                      MR. WAI

Pounds?

                          IGO

Common, I mean *nera*.

                      MR. WAI

Oops! Really too bad.

What if I show you a way

To make as much as twenty thousand pounds

In one day,

Would you allow me?

IGO

(Amazed)

Are you nuts?

Twenty thousand pounds?

MR. WAI

Yes, for something that will cost you almost nothing.

IGO

(Beaming with smile)

Twenty thousand pounds in one day?

Talk to me.

You know you are my very good friend.

GRADE VI

MR. WAI facing HASA. Both are on their feet.

HASA

(Harshly)

Kai! I am responsible for the gold portion of Engee,

But I dare not introduce that part to you

Without the consent of my brothers

Even though I am in control of it.

MR. WAI

(Convincingly)

If you'd ask me,

Doing it all

And taking it all

Is not a bad thing,

Think about it;

You have just two days

To get back to me.

GRADE VII

Same day. MR. WAI facing BENI. Both are sitting, eating chopped pawpaw from a tray placed on the table. MR WAI eats with a fork and knife while BENI eats with bare hand.

MR. WAI

(Persuasively)

You've got bronze and beautiful beads,

With a great many artifacts.

Wouldn't you rather

For hundreds of millions

Trade those mere artifacts

And be the boss of your own?

                    BENI

                    (Astonished, stammering)

Are you sure you know what you are saying?

You've got no palm wine in front of you,

So, you must be alright.

                    MR. WAI

Why not?

I mean what I've said

And I've said what I mean.

                    BENI

Hundreds of millions?

                    MR. WAI

                    (Nods slowly)

Yeah.

(BENI sighs deeply and becomes pensive, fidgeting with the pawpaw in his hand.)

GRADE VIII

HASA oscillating the stage pensively and panting.

HASA

(Soliloquizing)

That is huge money,

So huge;

It'd change my entire life,

But yes, I am responsible

For the gold portion of the land,

But do I do this behind my brothers?

(Brief pause)

Yes, we are blessed with other resources!

Now I am at peace,

We've got crude oil

And other precious minerals in the soil.

We'd lose nothing much.

Now that I know,

I should go for my lunch

No sooner than pretty soon.

It is I who shall be launched

Into stupendous wealth.

(Laughs out loud, proudly)

GRADE IX

MR. WAI sitting on a chair with a table in front of him. He is writing keenly.

(Voice-over)

To Her Royal Majesty,

Queen for the Colored World,

I have decided to continue from where I stopped,

And like I have mentioned before,

We shall eventually get them drained off completely.

Not only would we seize all precious substances,

But we shall also put them in eternal slavery

Like we have planned to do in other lands.

This is a nice domain for us

I must mention.

The Black People are quite aggressive but so united

That nothing but greed alone could tear them apart.

They are people who love entertainment;

In fact, they use that to avoid having to think deeply about life

And its sufferings and offerings.

Greed will also cause them in the long run to monetize their children.

I tell you Queen;

When promised other benefits apart from money

In return for their resources,

They began to succumb.

Hasa loves to be in charge

Of things, no matter how little it might be.

As I write in this diary,

I am yet to totally find out

Other things to use as baits

For others;

I will definitely get to know their weaknesses in few days

Before I finally approve the land for invasion,

Total exploration and exploitation.

I will journal again

Once I know something.

Your Loyal Explorer,

Mr. Wai Overseas.

GRADE X

MR. WAI standing with one hand in pocket in solitude, gazing at his wristwatch at intervals. Soon, KOG enters carefully looking around until he reaches MR. WAI.

MR. WAI

Kog, my very good friend.

How are you today?

KOG

(Huskily)

Look here Mr. Wai,

Forget about how I am.

All I can tell you now is,

I am ready to sell!

MR. WAI

(Excited, applauds)

You are ready!

Very good, you're just one step away.

You follow me and sign on a material

And that is it.

KOG

(Curiously)

Okay… Then how and when do I receive the money?

MR. WAI

(Draws closer and taps KOG softly)

I've got that covered.

You need not worry over that,

Let's go to my place

And we sort things out immediately.

KOG

(Shrugs)

I trust you.

(MR. WAI and KOG both leave the stage.)

GRADE XI

YOBA hurries to the center stage, facing the audience. Speaks in his unique native language, with gesticulation.

YOBA

We are so blessed that

It's not too bad to lend a helping hand,

To give little portions of our resources

To a stranger.

Loving your neighbor

Means to give out something little

That will cause you a little pain.

But since there's a gain for the pain,

Why not bear the pain a little?

Money makes the world go round.

Now, I am wiser and richer than my brothers!

You, walk a while in my shoe–

If you, I mean you–

If you had the chance to change your life story forever,

Wouldn't you do the same?

(Exits)

(IGO, HASA, BENI and KOG in turn hurry to the centre stage, facing the audience. Speak in their unique native languages, with gesticulation, and exit.)

GRADE XII

ENGEE lying flat on the mat in deep agony. She struggles to speak.

ENGEE

My compatriots have because of greed

Become a shadow of their rainbow,

What a pity.

The defender has become the oppressor;

They have sold me off

To foreigners forever.

If only they did unite,

They would make me great

And their greatness would

Forever be felt,

Not only among the other Black nations,

But also, in the eternal heart of the universe.

They have drained me off with no consent;

All that I have

Is taken away from me,

The river is divided

The oppressors have invaded.

(Engee gasps for breath till absolute silence is heard.)

EPILOGUE

NARRATOR enters. Hands folded behind him. He parades the stage twice, pitifully.

NARRATOR

(Solemnly)

Motherhood,

The source of your livelihood!

Motherhood,

Nurtured you

From childhood

To adulthood.

Brought brotherhood

To your neighborhood,

To make you learn and earn

From the power of cooperation,

To make you as strong as the hardest metal,

But you stooped so low

That you ash as mere wood.

Only if you had opened your hearts

To yourselves

Would you have been more closely knitted.

Only if you'd united

Fiercely and fearlessly,

You'd have defeated

The strange feet

That had stepped in

To the street of motherland.

I am at a loss for words

Because there are no words

To describe someone not bothered

About killing his brothers and mother

With the sharpest sword.

I know nothing

Except one thing;

It is this:

When we don't unite,

We untie.

The End